RUBBER STAMP CRAFTS

Craft Designers
RICË FREEMAN-ZACHERY
BONNIE LEWIS
DEBRA PETKEVICIUS
GRACE TAORMINA

Contributing Writer
ART SNYDER

Publications International, Ltd.

Ricë Freeman-Zachery is a writer, teacher, and rubber stamp artist who teaches college English part time and writes regularly for the publication *RUBBERSTAMPMADNESS*. Her work appears on pages 24, 41, 44, 49, 52, and 54.

Bonnie Lewis, a prize-winning artist and crafts designer, is a contributing writer to *RUBBERSTAMPMADNESS*. Her work appears on pages 9 (Faux Postage and Stationery and Envelope), 36, and 46.

Debra Petkevicius is a rubber stamp artist, instructor, and frequent contributing writer and artist for *RUBBERSTAMPMADNESS*. She is a member of the U.S. Addicts rubber stamper club. Her work appears on pages 9 (Collage Postcard), 21 (Sun 'n' Surf Notecard), 28, and 31.

Grace Taormina directs the Creative Stamping Department at Rubber Stampede. Her responsibilities include design and development and publication of how-to manuals and books. Her work appears on pages 12, 14, 16, 18, 21 (Dinosaur and Pansy Notecards), 26, 34, 39, 57, 59, 61, and 63.

Art Snyder writes "The Stamper's Art" column for *RUBBERSTAMPMADNESS* and is a longtime feature writer for the publication. He also serves as a consultant to numerous art-stamp companies.

Susan Lindstrom is owner of the Paper Source, Inc., whose stores retail fine art papers and rubber stamp materials. She also teaches beginning and advanced courses in rubber stamping.

Technical Adviser
Susan Lindstrom

Photography
Sacco Productions Limited/Chicago

Photographers
Peter Ross, Rick Tragesser

Photo Stylists
Melissa J. Sacco, Paula Walters

Photography Production
Roberta Ellis, Paula Walters

Model
Karen Blaschek/Royal Model Management

Special Acknowledgement
Dee Gruenig

The brand-name products mentioned in this publication are service marks or trademarks of their respective companies. The mention of products in directions is merely a record of the procedure used and does not constitute an endorsement by the respective proprietors of Publications International, Ltd., nor does it constitute an endorsement by any of these companies that their products should be used in the manner recommended by this publication.

Following are manufacturers whose products are used in this book: A Stamp in the Hand, 20630 S. Leapwood Ave., Suite B, Carson, CA 90746; All Night Media, Box 10607, San Rafael, CA 94912; Emerald City Stamps, 7925 Annesdale Dr., Cincinnati, OH 45243; Graven Images, 4211 Seneca, Chattanooga, TN 37409; Hero Arts Rubber Stamps, Inc., 1343 Powell St., Emeryville, CA 94608; Leavenworth Jackson, Box 9988, Berkeley, CA 94709; Mars Tokyo, Box 65006, Baltimore, MD 21209; Personal Stamp Exchange, 345 S. McDowell Blvd., Suite 324, Petaluma, CA 94954; Portfolio, 11 Roosevelt Ave., Westwood, NJ 07675; Posh Impressions, 30100 Town Center Dr., Suite V, Laguna Niguel, CA 92677; Printworks, 12403 Slauson Ave., Studio G, Whittier, CA 90606; Quarter Moon, Box 611585, San Jose, CA 95161; Remarkable, Box 2004, Snoqualmie, WA 98065; Rubber Stamp Express, 1409 Kuehner Dr., Suite 205, Simi Valley, CA 93063; Rubber Stampede, 967 Stanford Ave., Oakland, CA 94608; Stamp Berry Farms, 1952 Everett St., North Valley Stream, NY 11580; Stamp Francisco, 466 Eighth St., San Francisco, CA 94103; Stamp Oasis, 4750 W. Sahara Ave., Suite V-17, Las Vegas, NV 89102; Stampa Barbara, 505 Paseo Nuevo, Santa Barbara, CA 93101; Stampendous, 1357 S. Lewis St., Anaheim, CA 92805; Stampinks Unlimited, Box 97, Shortsville, NY 14548; The Rubber Room, Box 7149, Redwood City, CA 94063-7149; Visions of Ink, Box 133, Sisters, OR 97759.

Copyright © 1994 Publications International, Ltd. All rights reserved. This book may not be reproduced or quoted in whole or in part by mimeograph or any other printed or electronic means, or for presentation on radio, television, videotape, or film without written permission from:

Louis Weber, C.E.O.
Publications International, Ltd.
7373 N. Cicero Ave.
Lincolnwood, IL 60646

Permission is never granted for commercial purposes.

Manufactured in the USA.

8 7 6 5 4 3 2

ISBN 0-7853-0827-X

Contents

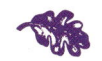   

Introduction
4

Special Delivery
Faux Postage • Collage Postcard • Stationery and Envelope
9

Noel
Gift Wrap and Gift Tag
12

Fruitful Endeavor
Gift Wrap and Gift Tag
14

Oak Leaves
Gift-wrap Wreath
16

It's in the Bag
Anniversary Gift Bag and Gift Tag • Halloween Goodie Bag
18

Picture Perfect
Photo-frame Notecards
21

What's Cookin'?
Recipe Cards from Hand-carved Stamps
24

Quilting Bee
Notecard
26

Moovin' On
Interactive Notecard
28

Dropping a Line
3-D Notecard
31

Festive Occasion
Contour Card
34

Happy Graduation
Five-panel Contour Card
36

One Lump or Two?
3-D Party Invitation
39

Easter Greetings
3-D Pop-up Card
41

From the Heart
Accordion-fold Book
44

Isn't It Romantic?
Lantern Card
46

Little Treasure
Shaker Jewel Box
49

High Noon
Polymer-clay Earrings and Pin
52

Charming Kitten
Polymer-clay Necklace
54

Painted Desert
Terra-cotta Clay Pot
57

Safari
Framed Picture
59

Holiday Spirit
Christmas Stocking
61

Tee-rific!
Birthday T-shirt
63

Introduction

Graphic designers, illustrators, painters, and printmakers the world over rejoice in the use of rubber stamps, and no wonder. Stamping is quick, fun, easy, and versatile, giving the artist a full range of creative expression.

For the beginning rubber stamp artist, stamps are an entrée into the realm of imagination. You can create your own greeting cards, stationery, wrapping paper, fabric designs—even jewelry!

It takes very little to get started. Your enthusiasm and artistic sensibility are a large part of the picture. You don't have to know how to draw, and you don't need a fine-arts degree. All you need is a few stamps, ink pads, papers, and accessories, and you're on your way.

But first, take a few moments to learn the basics of stamping. Once you read the sections on Getting Started, Tools and Accessories, and Techniques, you'll quickly be able to create projects as handsome and professional looking as those featured on the following pages.

GETTING STARTED

Rubber stamps. Start your collection of rubber stamps with images for a variety of settings. Stars, balloons, and other festive images are a must, whether you want to jazz up your mail, make jewelry, brighten up a T-shirt, or create an anniversary card. Word stamps like "Hooray!," "Thank You," and "Congratulations" always are useful. You may have a strong interest in teddy bears, cats, hearts, flowers, or other items. If so, consider building your collection from one of these starting points.

Look for two general styles of images: solid and line-art. A solid image lets you quickly get a lot of color onto a surface. Just a tap on an ink pad will do. In many ways, solid images recall bold prints made with linoleum blocks, woodcuts, and wood engravings. A line-art image may look like cartoon art or a fine pen-and-ink drawing. Either way, this design style shows the outline and details of an image, rather than a solid mass. Once it's inked and stamped on a surface, the impression is ready for hand coloring with pencils or markers.

Try to see the potential in every image you add to your stamp collection. Often, you'll want to combine two or more images. For example, if you're depicting fanciful flying dogs and cats, it's easy to do with the right stamps. You'll need conventional animal images plus a couple of wing stamps—just stamp the animals and add the wings. (If you bought stamps of winged animals, you'd be able to use them only as, well, winged animals.)

Inks. Begin with ink pads that use standard, dye-based ink. These are water-based inks; **never** use permanent inks for the projects described in this book.

Dye-based inks are easy to use, and the ink dries quickly. This type of ink pad is sold everywhere and comes in dozens of colors—you should have it in black, brown, red, green, blue, purple, pink, and orange. Add other dye-based colors and shades as you progress.

Pigment ink is thick, opaque, and slow-drying—not good for slick surfaces, but perfect for embossing. Pigment ink also works well when stamping on colored paper, because the color of the paper won't show through or alter the color of the overlying ink. When you need to stamp in metallic colors like gold, silver, or copper, pigment inks are unequaled.

Rainbow ink pads add an extra dimension. Instead of being just one color, they're multicolored. A single pad will have three or more different colors, usually in a striped arrangement. Another type has several shades or tints of the same color. In any case, a quick tap on a rainbow pad gives you instant, kaleidoscopic color. The pads come in both dye-based and pigment inks.

Papers. Begin with several types of white and light-colored matte papers with smooth surfaces. Try to get paper that doesn't bleed when you stamp it (unless of course you want a fuzzy effect). Dark or textured paper is suitable only in rare cases—for example, when stamped with metallic ink and embossed or when embellished with glitter paint.

Once you have your basic papers, you should consider specialty papers. These include glossy, matte, and coated stock and come in a range of colors and weights. Some work better with dye-based ink, others with pigment ink. Laser paper, for example, is great when you want a satin-smooth matte paper that takes a sharp impression. Marbled, handmade, and other exotic papers have their special uses and appeal.

Do you need heart-shaped cards? blank greeting cards and envelopes? Craft stores, stationers, and rubber stamp retailers, including many mail-order companies, often sell handy die-cut or scored cards and companion envelopes. They're worth checking out.

You also need ordinary scrap paper (low-priced typing or computer paper works well, too). You'll use it to see how your stamps print; to test all your inks; to experiment with techniques; and to make preliminary designs for projects. And save old newspapers, too—you'll need them to protect your work area as you stamp.

TOOLS AND ACCESSORIES

The right equipment can put you in stamper's paradise. Your tasks will go more easily and look better if you have a good array of supplies. As you get more experience, you should have handy as many of these items as possible:

- Colored pencils
- Water-based brush markers*
- Embossing powders and embossing gun
- Glitter glue
- Scissors
- Pinking shears
- Glue gun
- Craft knives and cutting mat
- Brayer
- Fabric ink and marking pens
- Eraser carving material and carving tools
- Stamp positioning tool
- Cosmetic sponges

***Never** use permanent markers—they will ruin your stamps.

Tools and accessories: (a) colored pencils; (b) embossing gun; (c) water-based brush markers; (d) fabric ink; (e) glitter glue; (f) glue gun; (g) craft knives; (h) carving tools; (i) eraser carving material; (j) cutting mat; (k) scissors; (l) brayer; (m) pinking shears; (n) fabric marking pens; (o) cosmetic sponges; (p) embossing powder.

TECHNIQUES

No matter which stamping project sparks your imagination, you need to understand the basics first. Keep these five general tips in mind:

1. Know the fundamental stamping variables.

The stamp, ink, and paper (or other medium) are most important, and each affects the other. Experiment every time you get a new stamp to see how it takes ink and leaves an impression. Check out its resiliency, and observe how it stamps on different papers or surfaces. Test new ink pads and papers as well. Different inks and brands of ink pads behave differently, and remember that various papers, fabrics, wood, etc., respond differently to stamping.

2. Learn how to ink a stamp on an ink pad.

Tap the stamp gently two or three times on a pad. Turn it over to see how well it's inked. Stamp it on scrap paper to get a feel for applying the right amount of ink to a die, or stamp. Too little ink causes details to be lost and colors to look pale, while too much obscures details. The image on new stamps usually needs heavier inking the first time around because the fresh surface is so porous. Never pound or rock a stamp when inking.

3. Perfect your general stamping technique.

Make a stamp impression by gently and evenly applying the inked die to the paper or other surface. Do not grind or rock the die (unless you're trying to achieve an unusual effect or are working with a curved surface).

4. Always work with clean stamps.

Clean off each die before you switch from one color to another and after you're finished using it. Follow these steps for cleaning:

a. Prepare a cleaning plate by moistening a paper towel, sponge, or small rag under warm running water, then wringing it out. Place it on a waterproof plate or in a shallow bowl.

b. After using a stamp, tap it several times on scrap paper to remove as much ink as possible, then tap it on the cleaning plate. Finally, tap it onto a clean paper towel or rag to remove moisture.

Never use alcohol-based solvents or other harsh cleansing agents—they can ruin a stamp.

5. Protect your stamps when they're not in use.

Store with the die side down, out of direct sunlight and away from dust. Lining your stamp storage container with thick construction paper is a good idea.

Inking and multicoloring your dies. You can ink a stamp in several ways. The easiest is to tap it onto a pad. Another way is to ink with a brush marker. This lets you color various parts of an image in different hues.

To do this, hold your stamp in one hand with the die facing you and color it directly with one or more markers. Work swiftly to keep the ink from drying out. When done, breathe gently on the stamp to generate more moisture, then stamp.

If you want to stamp only part of an image, hand-ink that portion with a brush marker, then stamp it.

You also can get a multicolored image by using a rainbow pad. When you ink an image on a rainbow pad, you get whatever colors the size of the image allows. A two-inch or wider image on a standard rainbow pad lets you get several colors with a single inking motion. A smaller image should be placed so that it straddles the division between two adjacent colors. This achieves at least a mini-rainbow effect.

When inking any image on a rainbow pad, tap the image several times **only in the direction of the color bands**. If you move an image perpendicularly, you'll blur the colors on your stamp—and your pad.

The "kissing" technique is an interesting variation. First, ink an image on a single-color pad, then carefully tip part of the inked image onto a pad of a second, darker color and stamp it.

(Kissing from light to dark ink avoids muddying your pads.)

Embossing. Embossing creates a stunning look, and it's essential to master. Keep these tips in mind:
- Use only pigment or embossing ink.
- Use only an embossing gun as your heating tool.
- Embossing thickens the line, so don't expect sharp images.

To emboss, ink the image on a pigment-ink pad and stamp it. Put a sheet of paper on your work area. Hold the stamped image over the sheet and dust liberally with embossing powder. Tilt the image so the excess powder falls onto your catch sheet. (You can return the excess to your powder bottle later.)

Remove the mask.

With the stamped sheet about six inches away, direct the hot-air flow of the embossing gun back and forth across the image until the powder melts.

Masking. Masking lets you add one image to another in a clever way. For practice, select an image to which you'd like to attach part of a second image. Stamp the base image on a sticky note so that some of the note's adhesive edge will remain after cutting out the image. This is your mask. Next, stamp the same image on a sheet of paper. Stick the cut-out mask on top of it. Stamp the same or a different image over the masked image so that part of it prints on the paper, part on the mask.

Stamp positioning tool. This helpful tool allows you to place stamped images precisely where you wish. First, stamp your image on tracing paper. Now, place a corner of the paper in the right-angle corner of the stamp positioning tool.

Remove the tracing paper and ink your stamp again. Place the stamp against the same right angle of the tool and stamp onto the surface, whether paper, fabric, wood, etc.

Remove the positioning tool.

3-D effects. Give your stamped artwork a novel look with 3-D techniques. One way is to stamp an image in one color, then stamp the same image in a second color 1/16 inch away. (Be sure to clean the stamp between inkings.) For that classic 3-D look, stamp the image first in red, then in light blue.

Shadows also lend dimension. With a wide-tipped gray marker, add a shadow to one side of a stamped image. (If you're doing several images in one scene, be sure all the shadows fall on the same side.)

Pop-up cards and decorative elements affixed with foam dots give a true 3-D look. See specific projects for detailed instructions.

Repeating. Repeat stamping, or successive stamping of the same image, is often used to create borders and show motion. For general repeating and for borders, you may use the same color each time, reinking for uniform results. (Try alternating colors for variety and rhythm.) To give the illusion of motion, ink your die once, then stamp the image repeatedly until the ink is gone. Keep each impression close to the previous one for that "zoom" effect.

Sponging and brayer inking. Use a small sponge to color backgrounds or broad areas. A cosmetic sponge dabbed onto an ink pad provides appealing texture.

A brayer works like a roller paintbrush. Run a brayer across an ink pad, then across your stamping surface for an attractive background.

(You can also sponge or brayer an entire surface, let it dry, then stamp on it.)

Following is a list of rubber stamp makers whose products we used in this book. Their names appear in the "What You'll Need" sections that follow, rendered in parenthesis as acronyms:

ASH (A Stamp in the Hand)
ANM (All Night Media)
ECS (Emerald City Stamps)
GI (Graven Images)
HA (Hero Arts Rubber Stamps, Inc.)
LJ (Leavenworth Jackson)
MT (Mars Tokyo)
PSE (Personal Stamp Exchange)
PO (Portfolio)
PI (Posh Impressions)
PR (Printworks)
QM (Quarter Moon)
RE (Remarkable)
RSE (Rubber Stamp Express)
RS (Rubber Stampede)
SBF (Stamp Berry Farms)
SF (Stamp Francisco)
SO (Stamp Oasis)
SB (Stampa Barbara)
ST (Stampendous)
SU (Stampinks Unlimited)
RR (The Rubber Room)
VI (Visions of Ink)

Order numbers, where available, follow the acronyms.

SPECIAL DELIVERY

FAUX POSTAGE • COLLAGE POSTCARD • STATIONERY AND ENVELOPE

Mail art makes keeping in touch a genuine pleasure. With the faux postage, collage postcard, and coordinated stationery and envelope, you'll make boutique-quality works of art. Friends and family will have as much fun getting news from you as you will mailing it!

WHAT YOU'LL NEED

FAUX POSTAGE

Square Postage Frame stamp (SB) • Brush markers, black and light orange • 4 × 6-inch glossy notecard, white • Sticky notes • Solid Blank Square stamp (RSE 442E) • U.S. Mail stamp (RSE 460F) • Glue stick ❧ Craft knife

COLLAGE POSTCARD

Postage-stamp-patterned tissue paper • Recycled-paper postcard • Glue stick • Uncancelled foreign postage stamp • Queen stamp (SO) • Brush markers, rust brown and ochre • Postage Circle stamp (RSE 476G) • Ink pad, metallic gold • Post stamp (RSE 482E) • Crown stamp (ECS 2537) • Cancellation Lines stamp (SU 2050C) • Ink pad, black

STATIONERY AND ENVELOPE

HooRah Lady stamp (QM RR102H) • Jumbo rainbow ink pad, primary colors • 8½ × 11-inch sheet matte-finish writing paper, white • Leotard Lady stamp (QM RR94E) • Aerobic Lady stamp (QM RR95E) • French Ribbon stamp (ST K19) • Square Blank Postage stamp (SB) • Matte-finish envelope, yellow

FAUX POSTAGE

1. Ink the square postage frame stamp with the black marker and stamp on the notecard. Surround the blank interior of the image with sticky notes.

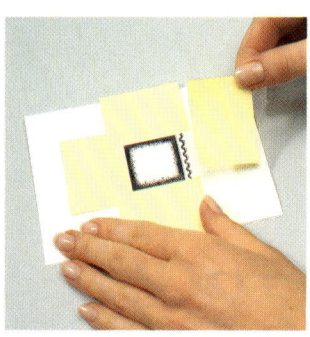

2. Ink the solid blank square stamp with the light orange marker. Stamp inside the already-stamped frame and let dry. Remove the sticky notes. Ink the mail stamp in black and stamp directly on the light orange image.

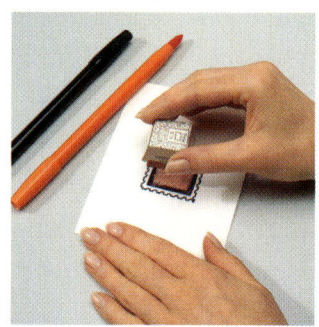

3. Cut out the faux postage with the craft knife. Create an adhesive surface on the reverse with the glue stick and affix to your envelope or postcard.

VARIATIONS

Try other stamps reminiscent of the art of letter writing, like the P.S. stamp and the rural route mailbox stamp. For ease in detaching and mailing, try stamping on perforated, gummed blank sheets.

COLLAGE POSTCARD

1. Tear the patterned tissue paper and glue it in place on the recycled-paper postcard using the glue stick.

2. Ink the queen stamp with the rust brown marker and stamp on the postcard.

3. Ink the crown stamp with the ochre marker and

stamp it randomly. Affix the uncanceled foreign postage stamp. Ink the cancellation lines stamp using the black ink pad and stamp on top of the uncanceled postage stamp.

4. Ink the post stamp in black and stamp in the upper-left and lower-right corners. Ink the postage circle stamp using the metallic gold ink pad and stamp it randomly on the postcard.

5. Stamp the postcard stamp on the reverse side.

VARIATIONS

You can vary this basic motif with different stamps, tissue paper, and foreign postage. For other variations, try stamping strawberries on white matte paper and accenting with red glitter, or stamping modernistic flowers on high-gloss card stock.

STATIONERY AND ENVELOPE

Making the stationery:

1. Tap the hoorah lady stamp on the rainbow ink pad and stamp in the lower-left corner of the writing paper. On a different part of the pad, ink the leotard lady image and stamp in the lower-right corner of the paper. Ink the aerobic lady stamp on the pad and stamp in the upper-right corner of the paper.

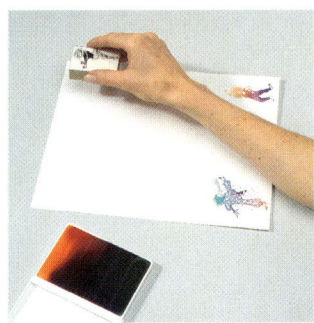

2. Tap the French ribbon stamp on the rainbow pad, then stamp three times each between the hoorah lady and the leotard lady; between the leotard lady and the aerobic lady; and to the left of the aerobic lady. (**NOTE:** Since you're reinking on different parts of the rainbow pad each time, be sure to clean the ribbon stamp thoroughly between impressions.)

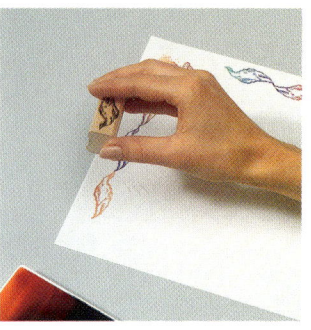

3. Reink the ribbon stamp and, starting at the hoorah lady's outstretched hand, stamp it four times going vertically.

Making the envelope:

1. Tap the square blank postage stamp on the pad and stamp in the upper-right corner of the yellow envelope.

2. Ink the leotard lady on the rainbow pad and stamp in the lower-left corner of the envelope.

3. Ink the French ribbon stamp on the pad and stamp once above and five times to the right of the leotard lady image.

4. Affix U.S. postage to the postage square when all images are dry.

Noel

GIFT WRAP AND GIFT TAG

Large or small, just about any holiday gift looks better garbed in radiant tradition. This season, bundle your gifts in an array of touch-of-gold holly leaves on high-gloss paper. A gold French wire ribbon completes the elegant look.

WHAT YOU'LL NEED

High-gloss gift wrap paper, white • Embossing ink and pad • Holly Sprig stamp (RS Z153-C) • Embossing powder, gold • French wire ribbon, gold • High-gloss gift tag, white ❁ Embossing gun

---

GIFT PAPER

1. Unroll enough gift wrap paper to cover your gift box. Working on one section of paper at a time, use embossing ink to stamp the gift wrap with the holly sprig stamp. Be sure to reink the stamp after each impression.

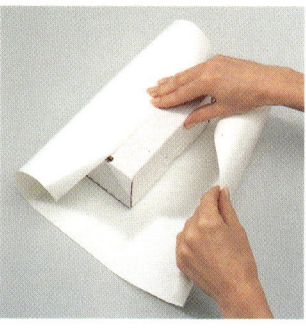

2. Sprinkle the images with gold embossing powder, tapping excess powder back into the jar.

3. Use the embossing gun to melt the embossing powder. Be careful not to burn the paper.

4. Wrap your gift and tie it with the gold French wire ribbon.

GIFT TAG

1. Stamp the holly sprig along the top and bottom edges of the gift tag.

2. Sprinkle with embossing powder and heat with the embossing gun as above.

See Introduction for key to rubber stamp manufacturer codes.

Fruitful Endeavor
GIFT WRAP AND GIFT TAG

A harvest of pears ripened with markers distinguishes your presentation. With smart raffia to complete this orchard, your gift is sure to say, "Open me first!"

WHAT YOU'LL NEED

Roll of kraft paper, brown • Pear stamp (RS A253-S) • Ink pad, black • Brush markers, ochre and light green • Raffia • Just For You stamp (RS Z404-C) • Scissors • Ruler • Pencil • Hole punch

GIFT WRAP

1. Unroll enough brown kraft paper to cover your gift box and cut with the scissors.

2. Ink the pear stamp with the black ink pad and stamp the kraft paper randomly, reinking the stamp after each impression.

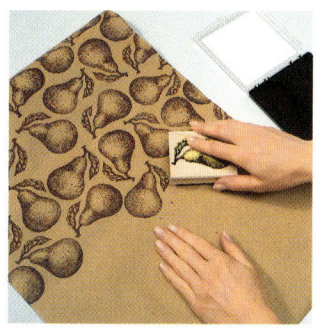

3. When the ink is dry, color the pears with the ochre marker and the leaves with the light green marker.

4. Wrap the gift and tie it with the raffia. Trim the raffia as needed with the scissors.

GIFT TAG

1. Measure with ruler and pencil and cut a 3½ × 7-inch rectangle out of the kraft paper with the scissors. Fold it in half to create a gift tag.

2. Stamp the pear and Just For You images. Edge the tag with the light green marker.

3. With the hole punch, punch a hole in the upper-left corner of the tag. Attach to the gift-wrapped box by stringing raffia through the hole and tying.

VARIATION

You can almost taste the crisp apples on this not-so-everyday lunch bag. From Maine to Washington, apples dress in delicious shades of red, green, and yellow, so try your hand in a grove of your creation!

Oak Leaves
GIFT-WRAP WREATH

This whirl of oak leaves provides an impeccable backdrop for a songbird in search of its golden nest. As a 3-D accent with rich embossing, this creation lends old-world charm to almost any gift wrap. A thank-you note is sure to follow!

WHAT YOU'LL NEED

Recycled-paper notecard • Oak Leaf stamp (RS 268-D)
• Brush marker, olive-green • Embossing pen
• Embossing powder, gold • Ribbon bow, gold
• Brass bird trinket
❦ Pencil • Embossing gun • Scissors or craft knife
• Low-temperature glue gun

---

1. Lightly draw a 2-inch circle on the notecard with the pencil.

2. Ink the oak leaf stamp with the olive-green brush marker.

3. Using the 2-inch circle as a guide, stamp the oak leaf in a circular pattern, overlapping the leaves slightly. Reink the stamp after each impression.

4. With the embossing pen, accent the outlines and veins of the oak leaves and sprinkle with the gold embossing powder, tapping the excess back into the jar. Heat the images with the embossing gun until the powder melts.

5. Cut out the wreath with the scissors or craft knife. Attach the gold ribbon bow and brass bird trinket using the low-temperature glue gun.

6. Affix the wreath to a wrapped gift.

See Introduction for key to rubber stamp manufacturer codes.

It's in the Bag

ANNIVERSARY GIFT BAG AND GIFT TAG
• HALLOWEEN GOODIE BAG

Decorative bags make carefree wrapping. Why not a glossy white bag with a bouquet of hand-stamped golden roses for a wedding anniversary gift? And for a real treat at Halloween, pumpkin images and embossed witch-black tissue paper make for a delightfully spooky goodie bag!

WHAT YOU'LL NEED

ANNIVERSARY GIFT BAG AND GIFT TAG

Rose Designs stamp (RS 771-H) • High-gloss paper gift bag, white • Embossing ink and pad • Embossing powder, gold • Tissue paper, white • High-gloss postcard, white • French wire ribbon, gold • Embossing gun • Scissors • Hole punch

HALLOWEEN GOODIE BAG

Lunch bag, white • Brush markers, orange and green • Plump Pumpkin stamp (RS Z282-C) • Index card • Ink pad, black • Tissue paper, black • Halloween Border stamp (RS Z361-F) • Embossing ink and pad • Embossing powder, gold • Ruler • Pinking shears • Hole punch • Wedge sponge • Embossing gun

ANNIVERSARY GIFT BAG AND GIFT TAG

Making the gift bag:

1. Stamp the rose stamp randomly over the front of the gift bag with embossing ink, reinking on the pad after each impression.

2. Sprinkle gold embossing powder on the stamped images. Tap the excess into the jar. Heat the powder with the embossing gun until it melts.

3. Repeat the embossing procedure for the tissue paper, stamping the two short edges of the tissue. (Be careful not to burn the paper with the embossing gun.) Insert the tissue in the bag.

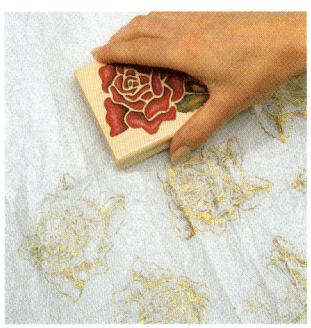

Making the gift tag:

1. Stamp and emboss a single rose on the postcard. Cut the image out with the scissors and use the hole punch to make a hole for the ribbon.

2. Attach the gift tag with the gold French wire ribbon and make a double-looped bow to trim the bag.

VARIATION

Adults will have as much birthday fun as a five-year-old with the medley of color in this variation on the anniversary gift bag. This is just the right setting for splashes of ribbon confetti and a "Happy Birthday!" salute.

HALLOWEEN GOODIE BAG

1. With the ruler, measure 5 inches up from the bottom of the lunch bag and cut off the top, using the pinking shears.

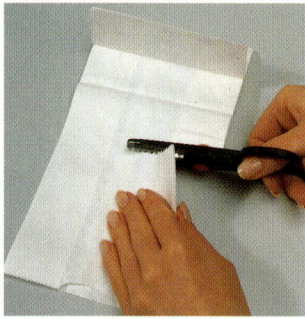

2. With the brush markers, apply ink to the pumpkin stamp, making the pumpkin orange and the stem green. Breathe on the stamp, then stamp pumpkin images randomly on the bag. Reink the stamp after each impression.

3. For the polka dot background, make a dot stencil by punching a hole with the hole punch in the index card. Ink the wedge sponge with the black ink pad and, using the stencil, sponge dots randomly all over the white bag.

4. Divide the black tissue paper into two parts. Ink the halloween border stamp with embossing ink and stamp the edges of the tissue paper. Sprinkle with the gold embossing powder, tapping the excess back into the jar.

5. Heat the images with the embossing gun until the powder melts. (Be careful not to burn the tissue paper.)

6. Insert the tissue in the bag.

VARIATION

Take youngsters back to prehistoric times with a selection of thundering dinosaurs in imagined colors. Finish off the bag with splashes of stars and stuff with festive ribbon confetti!

Picture Perfect
PHOTO-FRAME NOTECARDS

Here's a collection of photo-frame notecards with differing themes—dinosaurs, pansies, and sun 'n' surf—to suit the different moods of your photos. They're as much fun to make as they are to receive and display!

WHAT YOU'LL NEED

DINOSAUR NOTECARD

Photo-frame notecard, white • Dinobet Alphabet Kit (RS 935) • Ink pad, black • Stunning Stars stamp (RS Z275-B) • Brush markers, assorted bright colors

❊ Metal ruler

PANSY NOTECARD

Pansy Blossom stamp (RS 308-C) • Ink pad, fuchsia • Piece of paper • Photo-frame notecard, white • Fine-point brush markers, ochre, deep lilac, light green, and dusty pink

SUN 'N' SURF NOTECARD

5½ × 4¼-inch folded star-window notecard (glossy on one side) • Sheet of newsprint • New Waves stamp (PI 2412) • Brush markers, azure, yellow, orange-yellow, and orange • Sun stamp (SB) • Snapshot • Transparent tape

❊ Scissors

DINOSAUR NOTECARD

1. Open the photo-frame notecard and lay it flat. Ink assorted dinosaur stamps with the black ink pad and stamp randomly on the face of the card.

2. Ink a single star on the stars stamp with a brush marker in a bright color.

Stamp between two dinosaur images and repeat wherever you want this particular color star to appear.

3. Clean the stamp and repeat with a different color brush marker and different size star, if desired.

4. Color in the dinosaur images with the assorted markers.

5. With the metal ruler as a guide, use a blue brush marker to add a border to the interior and exterior edges.

PANSY NOTECARD

1. Ink the pansy stamp with the fuchsia ink pad.

2. Insert the piece of paper between the front and back of the photo-frame notecard. Stamp pansies randomly on the frame of the card, reinking the stamp after each impression. Change the position of the stamp for variety, bleeding the images off the edge and center of the frame.

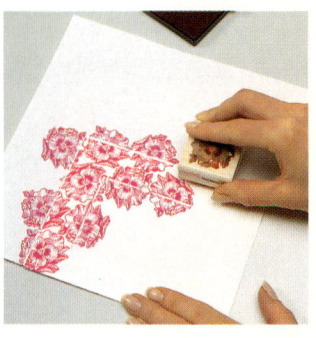

22 *See Introduction for key to rubber stamp manufacturer codes.*

3. Use the fine-point ochre marker to color the center of a few pansies, a few petals, and several whole pansies.

4. Color the rest of the pansies with the deep lilac marker.

5. Color the leaves with the light green marker.

6. Use the dusty pink marker to color the open areas of the frame.

SUN 'N' SURF NOTECARD

1. Unfold the notecard and flatten it, glossy side up, on the sheet of newsprint.

2. Ink the wave stamp with the azure marker and stamp across the bottom half of the star window until no ink remains on the stamp. Reink and repeat. For a flowing look, overlap the waves and bleed off the edges of the card.

3. Ink the sun stamp with brush markers, as follows: yellow in the center; orange-yellow around the center and slightly overlapping the yellow; and orange in the rays. Stamp in the upper-left corner of the card's face.

4. Hold the snapshot in the window. Center it, then trim any excess with the scissors. Turn the card over and affix the snapshot with the transparent tape.

23

WHAT'S COOKIN'?
RECIPE CARDS FROM HAND-CARVED STAMPS

The beginning stamp carver will appreciate this project—it's meant to look "primitive," as if the shapes came from a cookie cutter! With practice, you'll be able to create more complex stamp shapes, like geometric designs and flowers, but this gives you the solid start you need.

WHAT YOU'LL NEED

Tracing paper • Soft-lead pencil • Eraser carving material • Ink pad, dark red • Ink pad, dark green • Scrap paper • 12 4 × 6-inch cards, off white • Colored pencil, dark red • 24-inch length twine • Cutting surface or board • Craft knife • Linoleum cutter (#21 blade) • Ruler

---

1. Photocopy the tree and heart patterns on this page. Trace them on the tracing paper with the soft-lead pencil, then transfer them to the eraser carving material by placing the paper face down and rubbing the back of the image with your thumbnail.

2. On the cutting surface or board, cut the two images apart with the craft knife, then cut them out using the linoleum cutter. (As you cut, turn the carving material rather than moving the cutter.)

3. Trim away the excess from the two images with the craft knife, slanting the cut away from the image.

4. Using the dark red and dark green ink pads, test the images by stamping on scrap paper. Trim again if needed.

5. On each of the 12 cards, stamp the tree in dark green at each end and in the middle along the bottom. Stamp the heart in red between the trees.

6. Use the ruler and dark red pencil to mark off five lines a half-inch apart on each card, starting a half-inch from the top. If desired, mark off lines on the reverse, as well.

7. Bundle the cards and tie with the twine.

See Introduction for key to rubber stamp manufacturer codes.

Quilting Bee
NOTECARD

From "Congratulations!" to "Happy Anniversary!" an embossed notecard says it all. A stamp positioning tool helps you center the quilt star image on the card. Emboss in gold as you stamp out this display of tradition. A flourish of primary colors completes the message.

WHAT YOU'LL NEED

Folded notecard, white • Tracing paper • Quilt Star stamp (RS A257-H) • Embossing ink and pad • Embossing powder, gold • Sticky notes • Glue pen • Fine-point brush markers, red, green, and yellow • ✶ Craft knife • Metal ruler • Stamp positioning tool • Embossing gun

---

1. Use the craft knife and metal ruler to trim the notecard to fit your envelope.

2. Place a corner of the tracing paper in the right-angle corner of the stamp positioning tool. Ink the quilt stamp with any color marker, then stamp on the tracing paper, using the positioning tool.

3. Using the tracing paper, center the quilt star on the notecard. Place the positioning tool so that the tracing paper is in the right-angle corner. Remove the tracing paper.

4. Ink the quilt stamp with embossing ink. Guide the inked stamp into the corner of the positioning tool and stamp the image on the notecard.

5. Sprinkle with gold embossing powder and heat with the embossing gun until the powder melts.

6. Place a trimmed sticky note over the quilt image as a mask.

7. Using the tracing paper with the quilt image and starting at any corner of the card, position the tracing paper so that the center of the star is at the edge of the card's corner. Place the positioning tool so that the tracing paper is in the right-angle corner. Reink the stamp with embossing ink. Remove the tracing paper without moving the positioning tool and stamp the image.

8. Sprinkle with gold embossing powder and heat with the embossing gun. Repeat for the other three corners.

9. With the metal ruler as a guide, use the glue pen to add a border around the card. Sprinkle with gold embossing powder and heat with the embossing gun.

10. Color the design with red, green, and yellow markers.

See Introduction for key to rubber stamp manufacturer codes.

Moovin' On

INTERACTIVE NOTECARD

Moove over! Make way in your creative repertoire for this delightful card incorporating masking, glitter, and a sliding ornament. It's a perfect way to say hello to your newly relocated friend or relative.

WHAT YOU'LL NEED

3 5½ × 4¼-inch folded notecards (glossy on one side)
• House stamp (ECS 2916) • Brush markers, turquoise, green, dark green, yellow, orange-yellow, orange, baby blue, azure, and black • Sheets of newsprint • Hilltop stamp (PI Z251E) • Clump of Grass stamp (PR A899) • Sun stamp (SB) • Cluster of Clouds stamp (ANM 452E) • Sparrow stamp (Garden Set stamps by PSE) • Small flower stickers • Cow stamp (ANM 165D) • 1½ × 2-inch sticky notes • Fine-point marker, black • Rubber cement • 3¼ × ¾-inch strip poster board • Mounting tape • Dialog Bubble stamp (PI Z277E) • Clear glitter glue
✾ Craft knife • Scissors

---

1. Unfold one notecard and flatten it, glossy side up.

2. Ink the house stamp with the turquoise marker and stamp it in the lower-right corner.

3. Place the notecard on a sheet of newsprint. Ink the hilltop stamp with the green marker and stamp it repeatedly in the lower third of the notecard until no ink remains on the stamp. For a flowing look, overlap the hilltops and bleed off the edges of the notecard. Repeat, inking the hilltop stamp with the dark green marker.

4. Ink the grass-clump image with the dark green marker and randomly stamp on the hilltop images.

5. Ink the sun image with markers, as follows: yellow in the center; orange-yellow around the center and slightly overlapping the yellow; and orange in the rays. Stamp in the top center of the notecard.

6. Ink the cloud stamp with the baby blue marker. Stamp it once on newsprint, then repeatedly in the upper third of the card until no ink remains.

7. Ink the sparrow stamp with the azure marker and stamp twice in the sky, with the left-hand image bleeding off the left edge of the card.

8. With the craft knife, cut a 3-inch slit beginning ¾ inch from the left edge of the card and ¾ inch from the bottom edge. Cut a second slit 2 inches above and parallel to the first.

9. Place flower stickers randomly among the grass images and set the card aside.

10. Ink the cow stamp with the black marker and stamp it on the second notecard. Immediately stamp the cow again on a sticky note close to the adhesive edge. With the scissors, cut out the image to create a mask.

11. Place the mask over the stamped cow on the notecard. Reink the cow image and stamp to the right of, and slightly overlapping, the center cow image. Repeat on the left side of the center cow. Remove the mask. Cut out the group of cows with the scissors.

12. Ink the cloud stamp with the baby blue marker and stamp on the second notecard. Cut out the large center cloud with the scissors. Using the fine-point black marker, write "Pull" and draw a right-pointing arrow on the cloud.

13. Place the notecard flat on newsprint with the house face down. Brush the wrong side of the card generously with rubber cement, **but not in the area between the two slits**. Immediately lay the third notecard on top of the wet surface, glossy side up. Press together for a firm bond.

14. Fold the card along the crease with the house side face up. Slide the strip of poster board between the two slits, leaving a short end extending out the bottom. With the mounting tape, affix the group of cows to the extended end.

15. Holding the cows in place, tape the cloud to the top end of the poster-board strip.

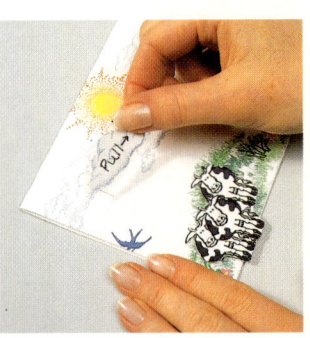

16. Open the card and, in black, stamp a cow and the dialog bubble on the inside right. Write "Hope you had a s<u>moo</u>th <u>moo</u>ve" in the bubble. Close the card. Dab the clear glitter glue on the sun image and let dry.

30

DROPPING A LINE
3-D NOTECARD

"Drop in" on friends or family with this cleverly crafted three-dimensional card. With its lush outdoor background and use of real twine and tiny clothespins, this piece invites an enthusiastic response.

WHAT YOU'LL NEED

2 5½× 4¼-inch folded notecards (glossy on one side)
• Sheets of newsprint • Hilltop stamp (PI Z251E)
• Brush markers, green, dark green, baby blue, yellow, orange-yellow, orange, black, red, and royal blue
• Cloud stamp (PI Z327C) • Sun stamp (SB) • Clothes Line stamp (VI 111G) • Bird stamp (RE 033A) • Flower stamp (ST AA48) • 10-inch length twine • T-Shirt stamp (SB) • Dot Letter Alphabet Stamp Set (HA)
• 2 miniature plastic clothespins, red
❧ Craft knife • Scissors

---

1. Unfold one notecard and flatten it, glossy side up, on a sheet of newsprint.

2. Ink the hilltop image with the green marker and stamp along the bottom third of the card. Repeat until no ink remains on the stamp. For a flowing look, overlap the hilltops and bleed off the edges of the card. Reink and repeat.

3. Ink the hilltop image with the dark green marker and stamp it repeatedly across the bottom third of the card until no ink remains on the stamp. Reink and repeat.

4. Ink the cloud stamp with the baby blue marker. Stamp it once on newsprint, then repeatedly on the upper third of the card until no ink remains. Repeat.

5. Ink the sun stamp with brush markers, as follows: yellow in the center; orange-yellow around the center and slightly overlapping the yellow; and orange in the sun's rays. Stamp in the upper-right corner of the card.

6. Ink the clothes line stamp with the black marker and stamp in the upper-left corner, bleeding off the edges of the card. Reink and stamp again, this time with the left end of the clothes line touching the first stamped clothes line and the right end extending off the card.

7. Ink the bird stamp with the red marker and stamp so that the bird perches on the clothes line.

8. Ink the flower stamp in orange and stamp in the grass. Reink and repeat as often as desired.

9. With the craft knife, make two ½-inch slits ⅛ inch apart in the upper-left corner of the card. Repeat in the upper-right corner.

10. Thread one end of the twine through the left pair of slits. Tie a knot in the twine to the left of the slits. Thread the other end of twine through the right pair of slits, picking up the slack. Tie a knot to the right of the right-hand slits. Trim the excess twine.

11. Set the first card aside. Unfold the second notecard and flatten it, glossy side up.

12. Ink the T-shirt stamp in black and stamp on the second notecard. Cut out the T-shirt with the scissors. One at a time, ink the appropriate letters on the alphabet stamps with orange, red, green, and royal blue markers, then stamp "DROPPING A LINE" on the T-shirt. (Clean stamps between impressions if inking the same stamp in different colors.)

13. With the red plastic clothespins, attach the T-shirt to the twine.

33

Festive Occasion
CONTOUR CARD

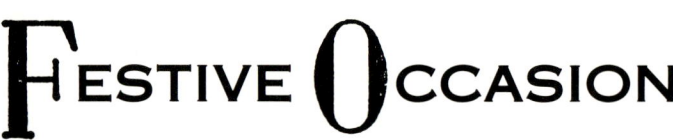

Balloons bursting with color mean only one thing—it's time for fun! Stamp your "Party!" image center stage and surround it with a chorus of balloons, streamers, and confetti. A contour cut along the balloon tops completes the magic.

WHAT YOU'LL NEED

Party Splash stamp (RS Z111-F) • Brush markers, fuchsia, red, blue, purple, turquoise, light green, green, pink, lilac, light blue, yellow, and orange • Folded notecard, white • Balloon Border stamp (RS Z427-F) • Sticky notes • Confetti stamp (RS Z173-C)
✄ Scissors

---

1. On the party splash stamp, brush-mark each letter with a different color: P - Fuchsia; A - Red; R - Blue; T - Purple; and Y - Turquoise. Color the splashes in assorted colors. Breathe on the stamp and stamp the image at an upward angle on the face of the folded notecard.

2. Begin stamping balloons closest to the word "Party!" Ink one balloon at a time on the balloon stamp. Starting with the long balloon at the left, apply light green ink over the entire balloon. Brush green on half the balloon and on the balloon string.

3. Breathe lightly on stamp, then stamp the image.

4. Clean the stamp thoroughly before inking a new balloon or switching colors.

5. Repeat the blending technique for the rest of the balloons, using the darker shade for the balloon string.

6. Stamp the individual balloons.

7. With the scissors, cut around the top edge of the balloons, leaving a narrow white border.

8. Open the card and stamp the round and heart balloons along the inside contoured edge. Finish stamping the star and round balloons on the facing side.

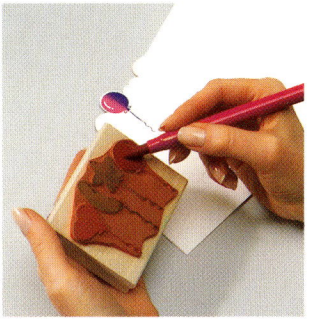

9. Stamp a star balloon and a couple of round balloons on sticky notes close to the adhesive edge. Cut out the images (balloon only, not string). These will be your masks.

10. Ink the confetti stamp in assorted colors. Place a mask over each balloon in the areas where you'll be stamping confetti.

11. Start stamping the confetti, bleeding the images off the top edge of the card.

See Introduction for key to rubber stamp manufacturer codes.

Happy Graduation
FIVE-PANEL CONTOUR CARD

Whether your graduate is finishing elementary school, high school, or college, this five-panel card is sure to please. The big, colorful balloons and confetti images add just the right note of celebration for this happy, happy, happy occasion!

WHAT YOU'LL NEED

11 × 17-inch sheet 10-point card stock, white (glossy on both sides) • Balloon stamp (SB) • Brush markers, red, orange, black, yellow, medium green, and turquoise • Fine-point marker, yellow • Happy (word) stamp (QM RR85D) • Alphabet Set stamp (GI 397U) • Confetti stamp (SB) • Jumbo rainbow ink pad, primary colors ❦ Ruler • Pencil • Craft knife • Cutting mat • Burnisher • Eraser

1. With the ruler and pencil, measure and lightly mark the card stock to make five panels, each 3⅜ inches wide. (Pencil two or three dots, not lines—when erasing later, you won't spoil the paper's gloss.) Trim the excess with the craft knife on the cutting mat. Use the ruler and the burnisher to crease along the marks. Carefully erase the pencil marks.

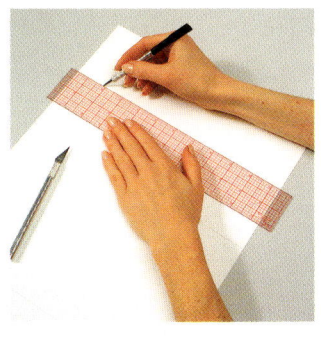

2. Ink the balloon stamp with the red marker and stamp on the left side of the sheet (panel 1), low enough so that the balloon string does not show. Touch up small blank areas with the fine-point yellow marker, leaving the center of the balloon blank. Clean the stamp thoroughly, then reink with the orange and black markers. Stamp on panel 2, a little higher than and at a slight angle to the red balloon, letting part of the string show. Repeat the yellow touch-up and clean the stamp.

3. Repeat the stamping procedure in step 2, reinking the balloon stamp with the yellow brush marker. Stamp it on panel 3 at a slight angle and slightly higher than the orange balloon just stamped. Repeat the yellow touching-up.

4. With the medium green and turquoise markers, repeat stamping the balloon image. The green balloon straddles panels 3 and 4, and the turquoise balloon is stamped on panel 5, a little higher than and angled to the right of the green balloon. Again, touch up with the fine-point yellow marker.

5. Ink the happy word stamp with the black marker and stamp in the blank center of each balloon.

6. Ink the alphabet letters for "HAPPY GRADUATION" in black and stamp across panels 4 and 5 under the turquoise balloon, leaving room for your signature.

See Introduction for key to rubber stamp manufacturer codes.

7. Tap the confetti stamp lightly on the jumbo rainbow ink pad. Stamp repeatedly and randomly around every balloon image. (Leave the signature area undecorated.)

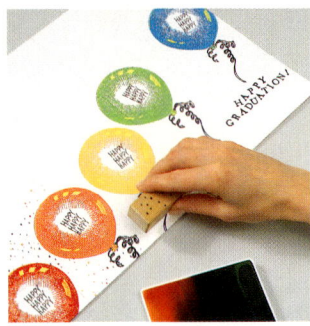

8. For the contour edge of the card, lightly pencil in the path you will cut on so that panel 1 is the shortest, panel 2 is a little taller, and so on. Trim with the craft knife on the cutting mat.

9. Turn the card over and stamp confetti along the contoured edge so that when the card is folded, confetti will be visible on panels 2 and 4.

10. Fold your card on the creased lines, with panel 1 folding to the left.

VARIATION

Try your hand at creating a scenic card, now that you've got the hang of making contoured panels. The variation shown involves nearly two dozen separate stamps, but not to worry! All that's involved is straight stamping and coloring in with markers—no masking, no stamp positioning, no enhancing.

38

One Lump or Two?
3-D PARTY INVITATION

Charm your friends with this debonair 3-D invitation. Party success calls for elaborate coloring of the teapot and teacup. Let stamped hearts abound, then contour the top edge of the card. Who can resist?

WHAT YOU'LL NEED

Brush markers, red, magenta, pink, orange, violet, light blue, turquoise, carmine, purple, pale violet, and bright yellow • Tea Cup stamp (RS Z474-H) • Folded high-gloss notecard, white • Posh Tea Pot stamp (RS Z473-F) • Sheet of newsprint • Heart Trio stamp (RS Z295-A) • You Are Invited stamp (RS 354-E) • High-gloss postcard, white • 2 foam dots • Scissors

---

1. Using brush markers in assorted colors, color directly on the teacup stamp. Breathe on it, then stamp the image along the lower edge of the folded notecard.

2. Using the same technique, apply assorted colors to the teapot stamp. Place the sheet of newsprint under the notecard. Stamp in the upper-left corner of the notecard, an inch from the top. Bleed off the edge of the card.

3. Using the heart stamp, select one heart and color it with the red marker. Stamp random hearts pouring from teapot to cup. Clean the stamp before changing to another color or using a different size heart. Repeat to complete the hearts pouring from the teapot.

4. Cut away the top edge of your stamped image with the scissors.

5. With the magenta and pink markers, ink the "You Are Invited" part of the stamp of the same name and stamp in the top right inside of the card.

6. Clean the stamp, then ink the "Why, When, Where" portion of the same stamp with the magenta marker. Stamp inside the card in the lower-left portion of the same page.

7. Reink the heart stamp and stamp random hearts in assorted colors as a border on the outside and inside of the card.

8. Reink the teacup stamp as you did in step 1 and stamp on the postcard. Cut out the image with the scissors, stick the two foam dots on the reverse side, and position directly over the previously stamped teacup for a 3-D effect.

VARIATION

Your guests are sure to arrive on time with this 3-D holiday invitation of evergreens and ornaments. Glittering globes on adhesive foam are an extra-special touch.

---

40   *See Introduction for key to rubber stamp manufacturer codes.*

EASTER GREETINGS
3-D POP-UP CARD

Although pop-up cards take time and require measuring, cutting, and scoring, the results are well worth it. They're perfect for any joyous occasion—not just holidays, but birthdays, birth announcements, and anniversaries.

WHAT YOU'LL NEED

4 6 × 9-inch pieces card stock, white • 7 4½ × ¾-inch strips heavy paper, 2 each in bright yellow and bright pink, 3 in purple • Double-sided transparent tape • Sun stamp (PO 231) • Cloud stamp (ST) • Jumping Hare stamps, left and right (PO 162 and 163) • Pigment-ink pads, black, bright yellow, bright pink, and bright purple • Colored pencils, yellow, orange, red, light pink, light blue, and green • Easter Egg stamps (PO 185 and 186) • Foam mounting tape ❋ Craft knife • Ruler • Cutting mat • Pencil • Scissors

Use the ruler and craft knife on the mat to cut these lines, making sure not to cut into the ⅛-inch margins left on the sides.

1. Fold two pieces of white card stock in half to make 4½ × 6-inch cards. Set one aside. On the other, make five pairs of cuts along the fold, using the craft knife and ruler on the cutting mat. Each pair should be a half-inch apart, with the distance between pairs varying. The cuts in each pair must be the same length, but the pairs should vary from ¾ inch to 2 inches long.

2. On the outside of the card, score the area between each pair of cuts by placing the ruler across it and rubbing lightly with the dull side of the craft knife. This dents the surface so that the card will fold more easily.

3. Open the card and weave the pencil underneath each of these pieces, pulling the supports toward the inside.

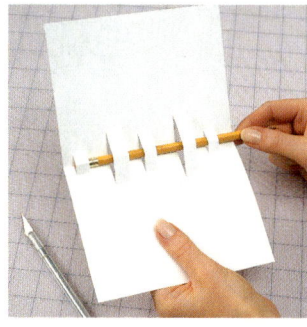

4. Slowly fold the card again, helping the supports bend inward. Crease and set the card aside.

5. Flatten out the second card. On the inside, use the ruler and pencil to draw five horizontal lines 5¾ inches long ¾ inch apart.

6. Weave the paper strips through these slits, beginning with one purple strip and starting at the outside. The next strip will begin on the inside. Alternate until six strips have been woven.

7. On the inside of the card, use your fingernails to pull all strips tightly together so that there is room to weave the last purple strip. Begin by inserting it in the middle, bending it if necessary to weave to both ends, but taking care not to crease.

8. On the outside, use double-sided transparent tape to secure loose ends.

9. Ink the sun, cloud, and the two hare stamps in black pigment ink. Stamp on the inside top of the first card, bleeding the clouds off the top edge of the card. When dry, color with colored pencils—light pink for the two hares, yellow and orange with red detailing for the sun. Outline the clouds with the light blue pencil and color the sky sketchily in the same shade. Color the inside bottom of the card lightly with the green pencil.

10. On the third, unfolded sheet of card stock, use the black pigment ink to stamp four left-facing hares and two right-facing ones. Stamp the egg stamps a total of ten times in bright yellow, bright pink, and bright purple pigment ink. Let dry, then cut out with the scissors.

11. Cut a 3 × 5¾-inch strip from the fourth, unfolded sheet of card stock with the scissors and place it over the back of the cut card. Secure with double-sided tape.

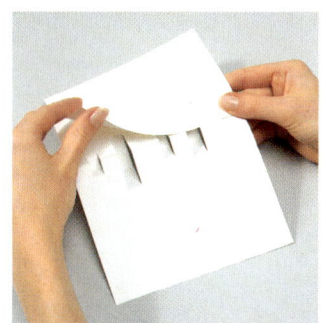

12. Attach the inside and outside of the card by placing strips of double-sided tape at the edges. (Don't put tape over the cut-out areas, or the card will stick together when closed.) Press together, matching up the edges. Trim with the scissors.

13. Stick some of the cut-out eggs on top of others with the double-sided tape or the foam mounting tape, depending on the depth desired. Tape these to the supports. Attach the cut-out hares to the inside top of the card with the foam tape, using double thickness where extra depth is preferred.

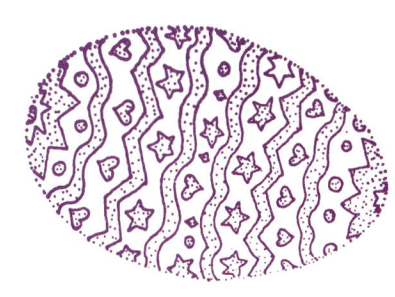

FROM THE HEART
ACCORDION-FOLD BOOK

Accordion-fold books can be made as simply or as elaborately as you like: You may want to stamp just the cover or every page. The finished product can be used as a keepsake or for addresses, photographs, poetic verse, and the like.

44

WHAT YOU'LL NEED

7 4½ × 9½-inch pieces heavy paper, red • Rubber cement • 2 4 × 5-inch pieces mat board, white • Pigment-ink pad, black • Hand Out stamp (RR 1277) • Heart stamp (SBF S43) • Pigment-ink pad, red • 2 18-inch lengths ⅛-inch satin ribbon, red • 8 3 × 4½-inch pieces heavy paper, white • Helping Hand stamp (RR 479) • Hold Hands, stamp set (RR 1102) • Open Palms stamps, left and right (LJ 5 and 6) • Cupped Hands stamps, left and right (LJ 446 and 483) • Thumbs Up stamp (LJ 423) • Double-sided transparent tape
✄ Scissors (optional)

---

1. Fold the seven red sheets in half lengthwise to make seven 4½ × 4¾-inch cards. Fit together to form one long accordion-fold sheet by inserting the edge of one card into the fold of another.

2. Separate the cards and apply rubber cement to all inside surfaces except the two end pieces. When the rubber cement is dry, fit the cards together as in step 1, making sure the edges line up. Trim if necessary with the scissors. Set aside.

3. Position one piece of mat board so that it is wider than it is tall. With the black pigment ink, ink the hand out stamp and stamp on the bottom third of the mat board. Ink the heart stamp with the red pigment ink and stamp on the fingertips of the stamped hand. This is the front cover.

4. Apply rubber cement to the inside of the front cover and the other piece of mat board, which is the back cover. Apply cement to the outside of the final two red pages.

5. Lay a length of red ribbon across the middle of each cover while the cement is drying. When dry, center the page ends on the covers and press.

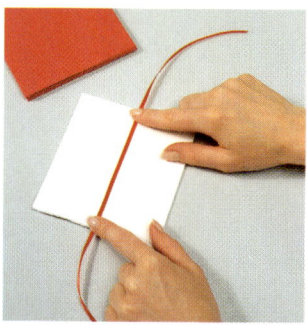

6. With the book folded, knot the left-side ribbons and tie a shoestring bow. This is the book's spine.

7. Fold the eight pieces of white paper in half to form 3 × 2¼-inch cards. Using the remaining hand stamps, stamp a different hand in black ink on the front of each card, then stamp the heart in red on each card.

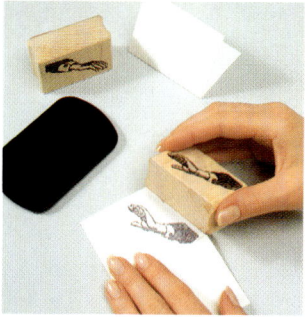

8. Attach a card to each page of the book, using the double-sided transparent tape. Vary the placement of the cards to avoid too much bulk in one place.

Isn't It Romantic?
LANTERN CARD

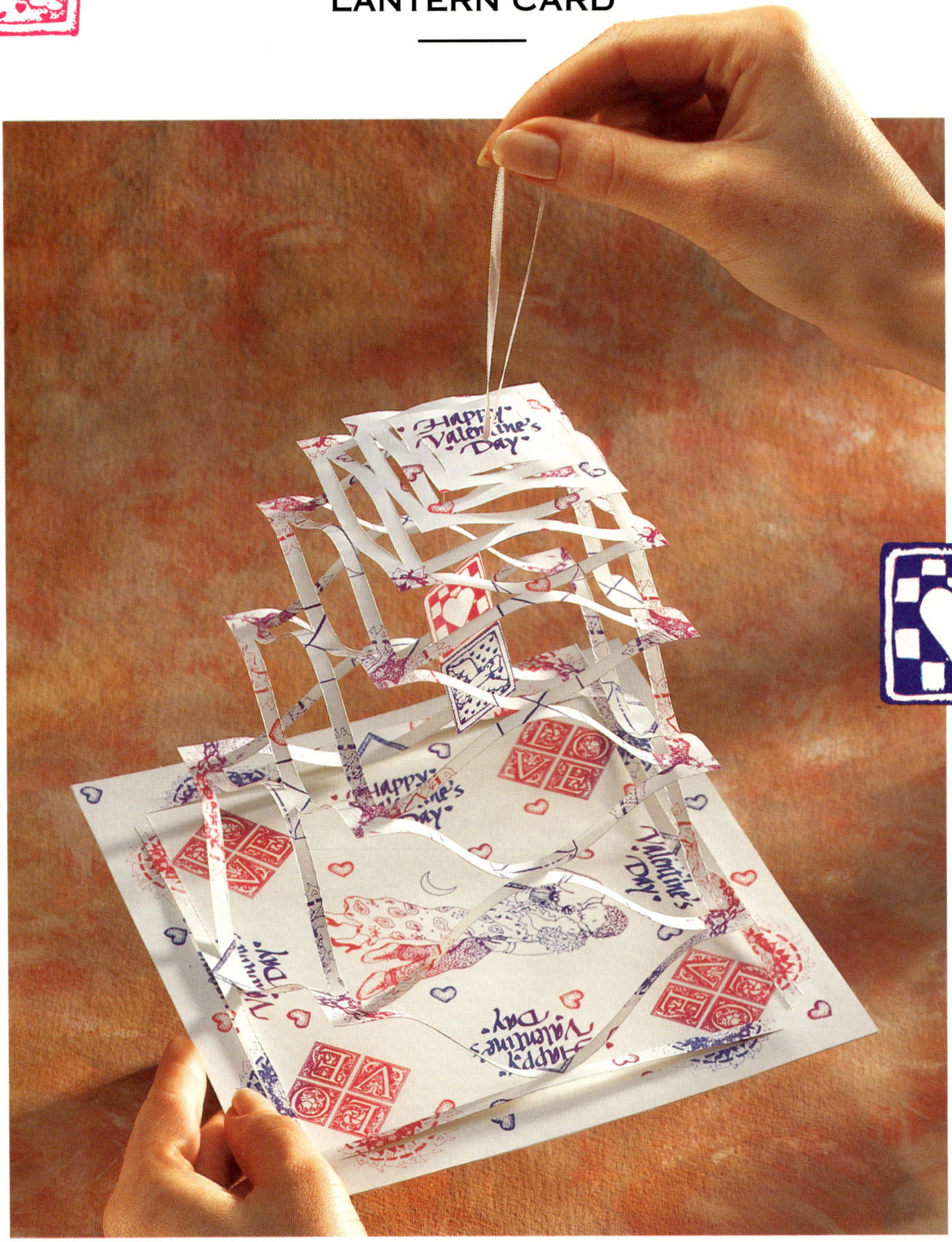

This visually delightful—not to mention tender-hearted!— lantern card is the essence of romance. Send it to your "heartthrob" on Valentine's Day, and you'll make a terrific impression!

WHAT YOU'LL NEED

8½ ×11-inch 7-point glossy paper, white (top of card) • Romantic Valentine stamp (PO G218) • Jumbo rainbow ink pad, shades of pink and blue • Open Envelope stamp (SB) • Happy Valentine's Day stamp (ASH C-195-KAT) • 8½ ×11-inch sheet 10-point glossy card stock, white (bottom of card) • Romance stamp (PO H415) • Love stamp (SF WO621-D) • Heart stamp (RE 106A) • Quilt Block stamps (SU L5-B and L6-B) • Double-sided transparent tape • 10-inch length clear plastic fishing line • 9-inch length narrow satin ribbon, pink • Single-sided transparent tape • Glue stick • Scissors • Cutting mat • Craft knife • Ruler • Hole punch • Large-eyed sewing needle

---

1. At a photocopier, enlarge the lantern pattern on page 48 to 7 inches square. On the 7-point glossy paper, photocopy this pattern, using the machine's manual feeder.

2. With the scissors, cut out the lantern pattern along its perimeter. Turn the pattern over and decorate the blank side as follows:

3. Tap the romantic valentine stamp on the rainbow ink pad and stamp four times, once in each corner. Reink as needed and clean the stamp between impressions if inking on different areas of the pad.

4. Ink the open envelope stamp on the pad and stamp once between each of the four impressions made in step 3. Reink and clean the stamp as needed.

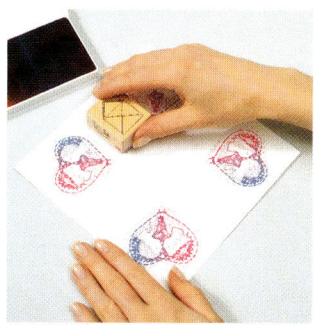

5. Ink the happy Valentine's Day stamp on the pad and stamp in the middle. Clean the stamp.

6. Using the pattern from step 2 as a model, lightly trace the square onto the 10-point card stock. This will form the bottom of the card. Cut out the square with the scissors and set aside. Save the scraps.

7. On the cutting mat, use the craft knife and ruler to cut along the black lines on the flip side of the decorated pattern.

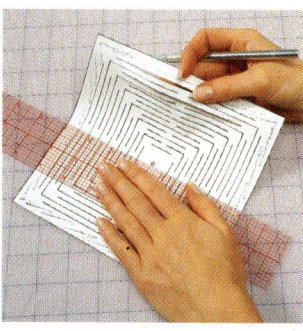

8. To decorate the bottom of the card, ink the romance stamp on the pad and stamp in the center. Ink the love stamp and stamp four times, once in each corner (clean between impressions if reinking on different areas of the pad). Ink the happy Valentine's Day stamp on the pad and stamp between each love stamp, reinking and cleaning as needed. Ink the heart stamp on the pad and stamp randomly, reinking and cleaning as needed.

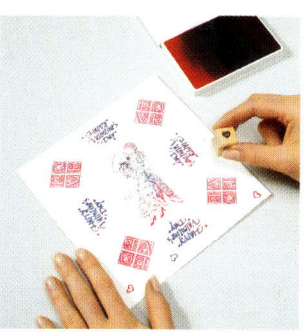

9. Punch a small hole in the dot of the pattern, using the hole punch.

See Introduction for key to rubber stamp manufacturer codes.

10. To make the dangling piece, ink the quilt heart on the pad and stamp it twice on the card stock scraps saved in step 6. Then ink the quilt bird on the pad and stamp twice, directly above and directly below the quilt heart images so that the images touch. Cut out with the scissors.

11. Stick the two images from step 10 together with double-sided tape, inserting the clear plastic fishing line at the top so that it is held in place by the tape. With the scissors, trim the edges of the dangling piece, as needed.

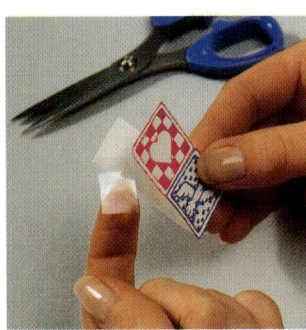

12. Thread the large-eyed sewing needle with the other end of the fishing line. Place the two ends of the pink satin ribbon through the hole in the pattern, leaving a six-inch loop at the top.

13. On the underside of the pattern, sew the dangling decoration to one side of the ribbon, then trim the ribbon and the fishing line with the scissors. Anchor the ends of the ribbon to the pattern with one-sided transparent tape.

14. Using the glue stick, apply glue to the edge of the card bottom, no more than a half-inch in from the edge. Carefully stick the top of the card to the bottom and press lightly. Let the glue dry.

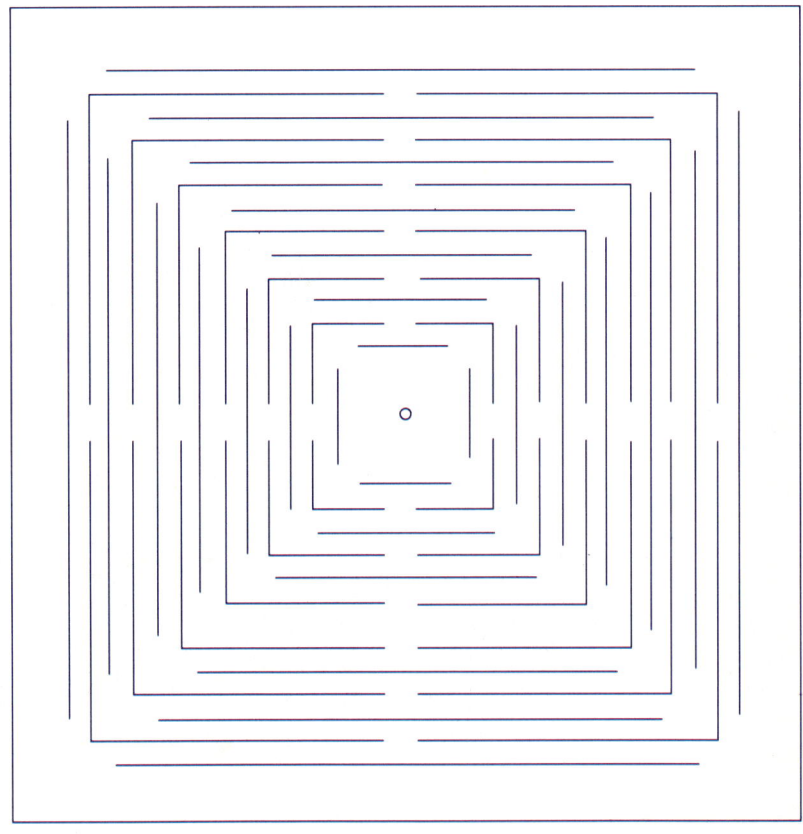

48

LITTLE TREASURE
SHAKER JEWEL BOX

With a little imagination, the right rubber stamps, and some pearls and rhinestones, Shaker boxes can be made as elegant as you like, serving as presentation cases, jewelry boxes, even gifts all by themselves!

WHAT YOU'LL NEED

Tracing paper • 5-inch diameter wooden Shaker box • ⅔ yard felt, white • White glue • Hand Out stamp (RR 1277) • Outstretched Hand stamp (MT 602) • Small hands, assorted (LJ 11B, 12B, 343B, and 900D) • Pigment-ink pad, black • Facial tissues • Ultra-soft colored pencils, assorted skin tones and red (or pink) • Spray fixative • Water-based varnish, clear • ½ yard ⅛-inch-wide satin ribbon, white • ⅝ yard imitation pearl garland (3mm beads) • 1 package half-pearls • 1 package 10mm×5mm acrylic faceted navettes, assorted colors • 1 package 5mm round acrylic faceted stones, assorted colors • 1 package 7mm round acrylic faceted stones, assorted colors

❋ Pencil • Scissors • Measuring tape • Small brush • Toothpick • Tweezers

---

1. On the tracing paper, trace the bottom and lid of the Shaker box separately in pencil. Cut out each circle with the scissors and place on the inside of the box and lid. Trim any excess with the scissors.

2. Measure around the outside of the box with the measuring tape and cut a piece of felt just slightly longer and wider. Use the tracing paper patterns to cut out two felt circles.

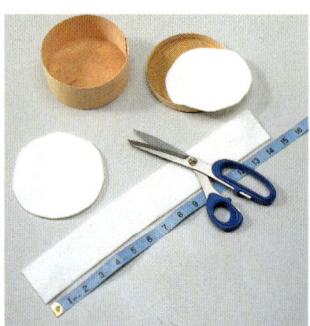

3. Fit all felt pieces inside the box, trimming as needed, then remove. Cover each inside surface with the white glue and press in the felt, smoothing evenly with your fingers.

4. While the glue is drying, start stamping the various hand stamps in black pigment ink on the lid and outside of the box. (The bottom of the box is round, so rock the stamps slightly.)

5. Let dry. If needed, remove any too-wet ink by pressing facial tissues to the images.

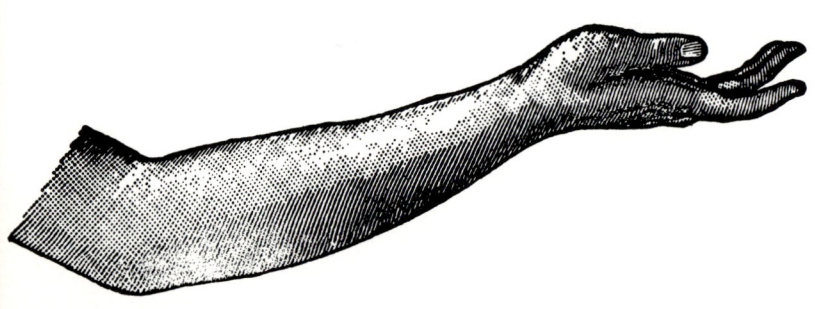

6. Color the hands in flesh tones with the ultra-soft colored pencils, then tip the fingernails in red or pink. Avoid coloring over the lines, as the ink might smear.

7. In a well-ventilated area, spray the box and lid with the fixative and let dry.

8. With the small brush, apply two to three thin coats of varnish to the outside of the box. Let dry between coats. Varnish the surface of the lid with extra coats for higher gloss.

9. Let dry, then attach the satin ribbon and pearl garland to the edge of the lid with the white glue, holding the garland in place until set. Trim the excess with the scissors. Cut 3 to 4 inches from the remainder of the pearl garland and glue to the lid. Hold in place until set.

10. Glue the half-pearls and acrylic faceted navettes and stones to the box and lid, applying the glue with the toothpick and placing with the tweezers.

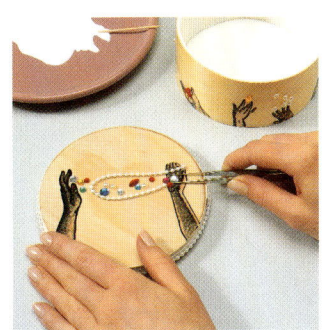

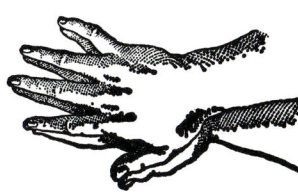

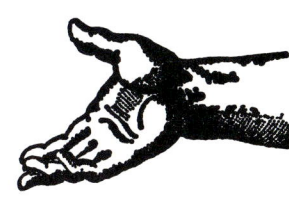

VARIATION

Shaker boxes lend themselves well to country images, like the cow-and-hearts motif. Even simpler to create than the jewel box, this variation requires cow and heart stamps, red satin ribbon, red felt for lining, and a miniature red bell to go around Bessie's neck!

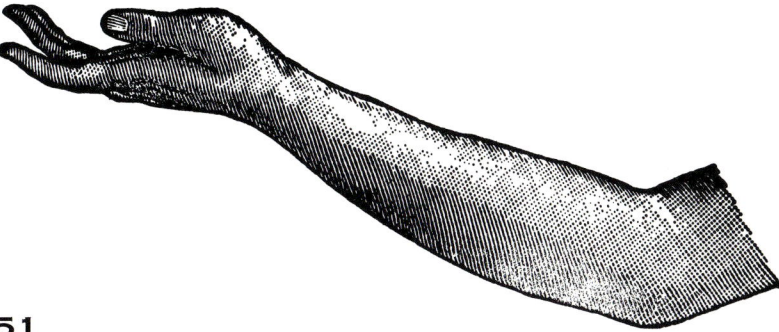

51

HIGH NOON

POLYMER-CLAY EARRINGS AND PIN

These easy-to-make polymer-clay earrings and pin only look ceramic! And the variations are limitless: You can use almost any stamp to create jewelry—bolo ties, hair clasps, button covers, even Christmas ornaments!

WHAT YOU'LL NEED

1 package polymer clay, white • Waxed paper • Sun stamp (LJ 234) • Pigment-ink pad, black • Aluminum foil • Facial tissues • Ultra-soft colored pencils, red, orange, and bright yellow • Spray fixative • Water-based varnish, clear • Gold-tone earring posts • 1-inch gold-tone pin back
❦ Rolling pin • Craft knife (#11 blade) • Baking sheet • Emery board • Cotton swab • Small foam brush • Hot-glue gun

---

1. Knead a 3-inch ball of polymer clay until soft, then on the waxed paper roll it out with the rolling pin to ⅛-inch thickness. Carefully lift up and turn over so the clay doesn't stick to the waxed paper.

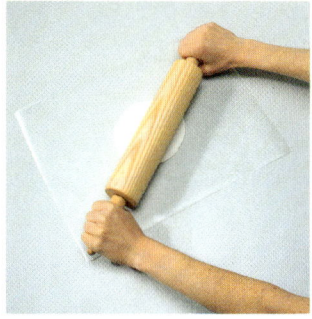

2. Ink the sun stamp with the black pigment ink and press into the clay. Repeat two times.

3. Using the craft knife, cut out each image as close as possible to the inked line. Avoid pulling the clay or cutting through the waxed paper. After all images are cut out, transfer them to the baking sheet lined with aluminum foil. Avoid smearing the ink or stretching the clay.

4. Lay facial tissues over the images and press gently to remove excess ink.

5. Bake 15-20 minutes at 250 degrees F. Let cool before handling. If needed, smooth the edges with the emery board.

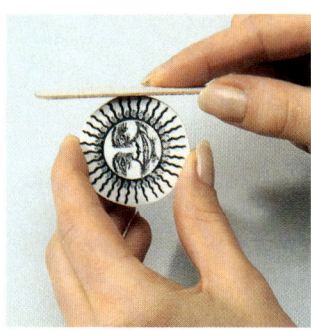

6. Color the lips with the red pencil, the eyelids orange, and the rest of the three faces bright yellow. Go over the cheeks in red and blend with the cotton swab. Color the rays with alternating lines of yellow, orange, and red.

7. Move to a well-ventilated area and spray each piece with the fixative. Let dry.

8. With the small foam brush, apply a thin coat of the varnish to the front of the pieces and let dry; repeat for the edges and backs. Add more varnish to the fronts for higher gloss, letting dry between coats.

9. Using the hot-glue gun, attach the earring posts near the top back edge of two pieces and the pin back to the same area on the third piece.

CHARMING KITTEN
POLYMER-CLAY NECKLACE

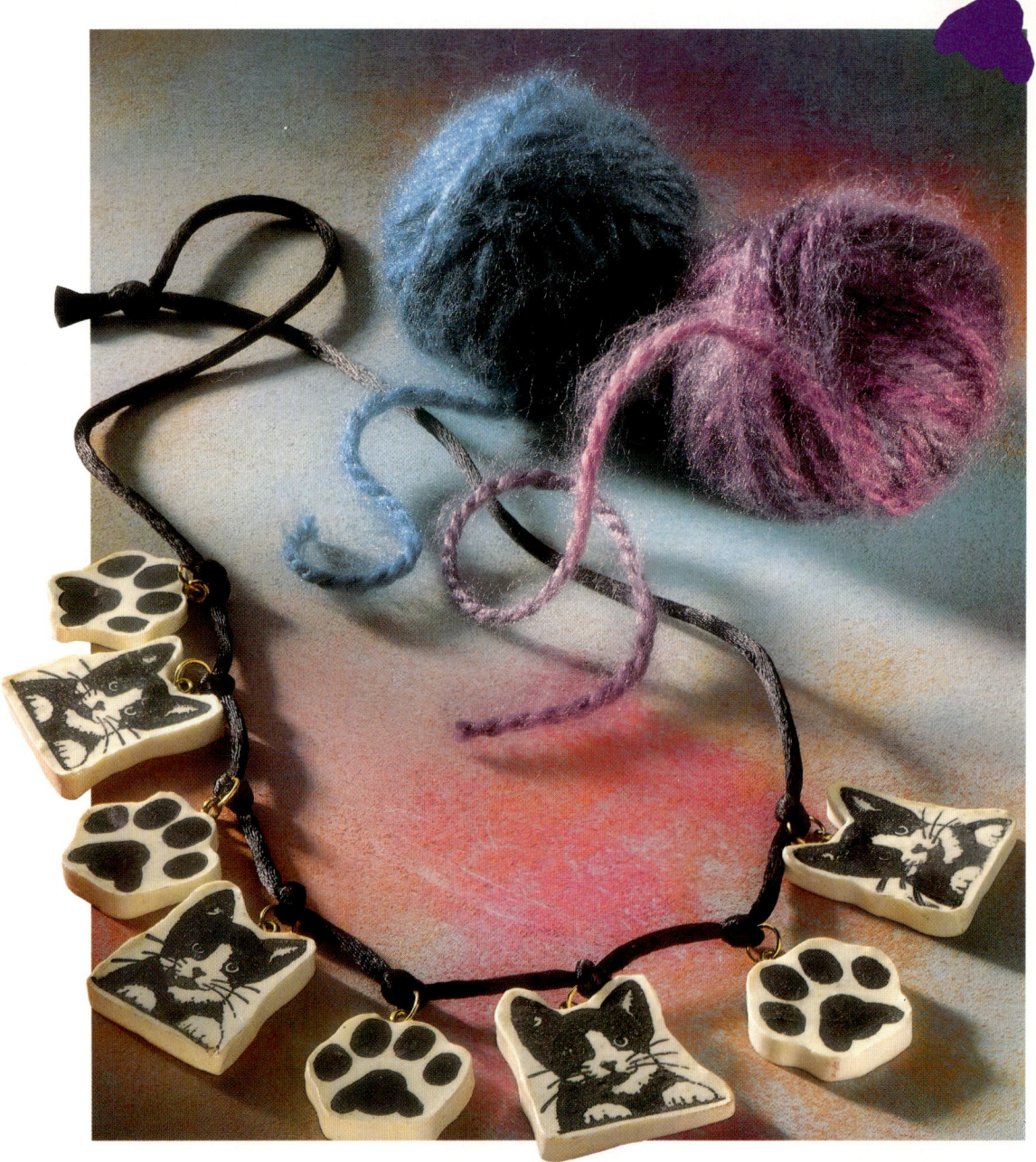

This whimsical charm necklace, made of polymer clay, takes a bit of time to make, but the techniques are simple, and the results will fetch a lot of compliments!

WHAT YOU'LL NEED

1 package polymer clay, white • Waxed paper • Lucky (kitten) stamp (ANM 226D) • Pigment-ink pad, black • Cat Paw stamp (ANM 221C) • Aluminum foil • Facial tissues • 8 small gold-tone screw eyes • White glue • Spray fixative • Water-based varnish, clear • 8 6mm gold-tone jump rings • 4-foot length rattail cord, black ❦ Rolling pin • Craft knife (#11 blade) • Baking sheet • Emery board • Small foam brush • Snout-nosed pliers • Scissors

---

1. Knead a 3-inch ball of polymer clay until soft, then on the waxed paper roll it out with the rolling pin to ⅛-inch thickness. Carefully lift up and turn over so the clay doesn't stick to the waxed paper.

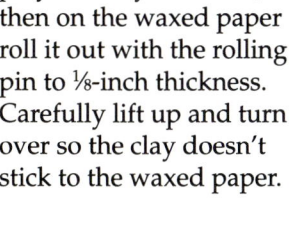

2. Ink the kitten stamp with the black pigment ink. Press it against the clay. Repeat three times. Do the same with the pawprint stamp.

3. Using the craft knife, cut out each image close to the outside line (don't pull the clay or cut through the waxed paper).

4. After all images are cut out, carefully transfer them to the baking sheet lined with aluminum foil. Avoid smearing the ink or stretching the clay. Lay facial tissues over the images and press gently to remove excess ink.

5. Carefully insert screw eyes into the top of the kitten heads and the top part of the pawprints.

6. Bake 15-20 minutes at 250 degrees F. Let cool before handling. If needed, smooth the edges with the emery board.

See Introduction for key to rubber stamp manufacturer codes.

7. Check the screw eyes by pulling gently on them. If any are loose, remove them and add a drop of white glue before reinserting.

8. In a well-ventilated area, place the charms face up on the waxed paper and spray with the fixative. Let dry.

9. Apply a thin coat of water-based varnish to the front of each charm, using the small foam brush. Let dry, then apply a second coat.

10. Apply several coats of varnish to the sides and edges of the charms, letting dry between applications.

11. Apply varnish to the front of the charms until glossy. Let dry between coats.

12. When the charms are dry, attach a jump ring to each screw eye using the snout-nosed pliers.

13. String a kitten about a foot from one end of the black rattail cord and secure it with a knot. Continue stringing the rest of the charms onto the longer end of the cord, alternating kittens with pawprints 1½ inches apart and knotting to secure.

14. Tie the two ends of the necklace together with a double knot after trimming the excess with the scissors.

PAINTED DESERT
TERRA-COTTA CLAY POT

*From cowpokes to cactus plants, the spirit of the great
Southwest is on your windowsill with this terra-cotta delight.
Gird the clay pot with rugged saguaros and top with radiant
suns along the rim. Raffia provides a rustic finish.*

WHAT YOU'LL NEED

Large clay pot • Paper towels • Acrylic spray, clear • Standing Saguaro stamp (RS Z239-D) • Radiant Sun stamp (RS Z165-C) • Scrap paper • Fabric inks and pads, emerald green and red • Double-sided transparent tape • Raffia • Scissors • Low-temperature glue gun

Caution: The clay pot is for decorative use only. Use artificial foliage, or insert a plastic pot inside the clay one if using live plants.

1. Wipe the clay pot with paper towels to remove any dust.

2. Spray the outside of the pot with the clear acrylic spray and let dry.

3. Stamp several saguaro and sun images on scrap paper, using the emerald green and red fabric inks.

4. Cut out the images with the scissors and use them as guides to determine the placement of images on the pot. Attach them with double-sided transparent tape.

5. Ink the saguaro stamp with green fabric ink and stamp on the pot, removing the paper pattern first. Reink and stamp the remaining saguaros.

6. Repeat for the sun image, using red fabric ink. Stamp only the top half of the image along the bottom edge of the rim of the pot.

7. Allow the ink to dry, then seal again with the acrylic spray.

8. Cut enough raffia to tie under the rim of the pot and attach it with the glue gun. Trim the raffia as needed with the scissors.

VARIATION

Using smaller or larger clay pots, you can duplicate the instructions above or choose different desert-motif stamps and different colors for variety. The clay pots are great for around the house—but also perfect for gift-giving!

SAFARI
FRAMED PICTURE

Capture the romance of the African savanna with these statuesque giraffes. Embossing gives them that gleaming look. Add ground cover and sheltering leaves for that realistic touch, then move on to picture-perfect framing.

WHAT YOU'LL NEED

Recycled-paper notecard • Giraffe stamp (RS 441-E) • Pigment-ink pad, black • Embossing powder, clear • Sticky notes • Grassy Meadow stamp (RS Z146-E) • Fine-point brush markers, ochre and olive • Spring Sprig stamp (RS Z250-D) • Mat board with 3½ × 5-inch opening, ivory • 5 × 7-inch wood frame, light oak ❋ Pencil • Ruler • Embossing gun • Scissors

---

1. With the pencil and ruler, lightly draw a 3½ × 5-inch rectangle in the center of the notecard. This will be your guide for placing the images.

2. Ink the giraffe stamp with the black pigment ink and stamp in the foreground of the notecard. Sprinkle with the clear embossing powder and heat with the embossing gun.

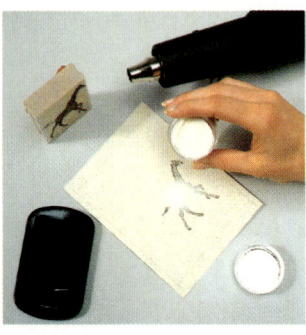

3. Stamp a giraffe on a sticky note close to the sticky edge. This will be your mask.

4. Cut the image out with the scissors and place it directly over the embossed giraffe.

5. Reink the giraffe stamp with black pigment ink and stamp to the left of and slightly above the first giraffe.

6. Remove the mask and sprinkle the second giraffe with the embossing powder. Heat with the embossing gun.

7. Make another giraffe mask with a sticky note and place the masks over both giraffe images.

8. Ink the grass stamp with the ochre marker and stamp over the lower part of the giraffe legs. Reink with the olive marker and repeat.

9. Ink the sprig stamp in olive and stamp on the upper-left portion and top edge of the notecard. Reink after each impression.

10. Remove the masks and color in the giraffes with the ochre marker.

11. Mount the notecard on the mat board and frame it.

VARIATION

The elephant picture is made using the same techniques—stamping, masking, and coloring in on recycled stock. Hung side by side with the giraffe picture, it creates a delightfully exotic effect for your walls.

HOLIDAY SPIRIT
CHRISTMAS STOCKING

Tangerines and holiday chocolates will taste even better when they're plucked from this cheerful stocking. Stamp the poinsettias, then embellish them with pine boughs. A gilded name and a dusting of gold complete the mood.

WHAT YOU'LL NEED

Several sheets of newsprint • Christmas stocking, white • Prize Poinsettia stamp (RS Z284-H) • Fabric ink and large pad, red • Plain paper • Double-sided transparent tape • Posh Pine stamp (RS Z151-C) • Fabric ink and pad, green • Dimensional fabric paint, gold-glitter • Ribbon, gold • Fabric glue • Bird trinket, brass ❦ Scissors • Small paintbrush • Toothpick

1. Place sheets of newsprint inside the Christmas stocking to keep ink from bleeding through. Stamp three poinsettias with red fabric ink.

2. Stamp a poinsettia on plain paper and carefully cut along the edge of the image with the scissors. This will be your mask.

3. With the double-sided transparent tape, stick the paper mask precisely over one of the stamped poinsettias.

4. Ink the pine stamp with green fabric ink. Stamp pines along the edges of the masked poinsettia, overlapping images for depth.

5. Remove the mask and repeat for the other two poinsettias.

6. Stamp a cluster of overlapping pine images at each end of the stocking cuff. Be sure to leave room for the person's name.

7. Use gold-glitter dimensional fabric paint to write the name between the pine images and to accent the pines with gold berries.

8. With the small paintbrush, accent each poinsettia with a touch of gold-glitter paint. Add dots of glitter paint to the center of each poinsettia.

9. Attach the gold ribbon with the fabric glue, using the toothpick.

10. Make a multilooped bow from the ribbon and glue it to center of the poinsettia cluster.

11. Attach the brass bird trinket to the cuff with the fabric glue.

VARIATION

The holiday aromas of oranges, cranberries, and pumpkin pie seem to be in the air with this exquisite lace placemat. A display of poinsettias on a bed of pine needles signals winter's joy.

TEE-RIFIC!

BIRTHDAY T-SHIRT

Presents, balloons, streamers, and party poppers—a white T-shirt is your canvas as you paint this celebration with your rubber stamps and fabric ink. Kids have a way of growing out of things—but this creation is sure to become a keepsake!

WHAT YOU'LL NEED

Child's T-shirt, white • Several large sheets of newsprint • Fabric marking pen • Posh Package One stamp (RS Z081-C) • Party Popper stamp (RS Z425-D) • Streamer Strands stamp (RS Z062-F) • Icing on the Cake stamp (RS Z205-E) • Fabric inks and pads, pink, red, purple, and green • Heart Trio stamp (RS Z295-A) • Balloon stamp (RS Z330-B) • Candle City stamp (RS Z206-E) • Dimensional fabric paint, silver-glitter • Big Star stamp (RS Z345-A) • Puff paint, red, blue, yellow, and purple • Fabric glue • Assorted rhinestones ❊ Steam iron • Ruler • Embossing gun • Toothpick • Tweezers

1. Prewash the child's T-shirt to remove any sizing, but do not use fabric softener. Iron the shirt to remove wrinkles.

2. Place sheets of newsprint between the front and back of the T-shirt to prevent ink from penetrating to the back of the fabric.

3. Using the ruler and fabric marking pen, draw an 8½ × 9½-inch rectangle about 3 inches below the shirt neckline. Divide the rectangle into four parts.

4. Using the fabric inks and pads, stamp one color at a time, reinking your stamps after each impression and cleaning stamps before switching colors. Stamp the package, popper, streamers, and cake in pink; the package, hearts, and balloon in red; the popper, balloon, and candles in purple; and the package, popper, and balloon in green. Allow the stamped images to dry.

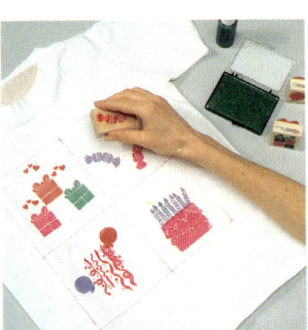

5. Draw the wavy border with silver-glitter dimensional paint, using the marker pen lines as a guide (the pen marks will disappear after a week). Paint freehand the balloon strings and the wavy lines above the candle flames with the glitter. Let dry for 24 hours. Then stamp the star image in pink in two rows across the T-shirt.

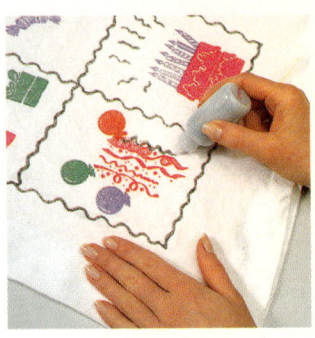

6. Apply puff paint to accent the stamped images. Use red for the hearts, package bow, and balloon; blue for the cake and package bow; yellow for the candle flames and popper; and purple for the package bow and balloon. Heat with the embossing gun until the paint puffs up.

7. Use fabric glue applied with the toothpick to affix assorted rhinestones, placing them with the tweezers. Let the garment dry at least 24 hours before wearing.

See Introduction for key to rubber stamp manufacturer codes.